LET'S EXPLORE THE CONSTRUCTION SITE

BABY PROFESSOR
EDUCATION KIDS

Speedy Publishing LLC
40 E. Main St. #1156
Newark, DE 19711
www.speedypublishing.com

Construction is the process of creating and building infrastructure or a facility.

Construction is managed by a project manager, and supervised by a construction manager, design engineer, construction engineer or project architect.

Construction workers do a wide variety of basic tasks. Basic laborers load and carry materials to the site, dig and fill holes, build scaffolds, and construct molds and bracing used for pouring concrete.

Construction workers use many types of tools and operate machines and vehicles such as trucks and bulldozers.

Construction workers have to wear safety clothing to protect themselves, such as leather work boots with a metal toe, plastic construction hats or helmets, and goggles to protect their eyes.

There are three sectors of construction: buildings, infrastructure and industrial. Building construction is the process of adding structure to real property or construction of buildings.

Infrastructure includes large public works, dams, bridges, highways, water and utility distribution. Industrial includes refineries, process chemical, power generation, mills and manufacturing plants.

Scaffold is a temporary structure used to support a work crew and materials to aid in the construction, repair of buildings, bridges and all other man made structures.

Crane is one very useful construction machine that can be found at every construction site, and can be used for different purposes.

The capability to raise and lower different kinds of loads and to move them horizontally, is the reason cranes are widely used machines.

Backhoe loader is one of the most commonly seen pieces of construction equipment. Backhoe loaders can be used for digging holes/excavation, landscaping, breaking asphalt, and paving roads.

Cement mixer trucks are used to transport and mix concrete up to the construction site. The cement mixer truck maintains the material's liquid state through turning of the drum, until delivery.

Construction is a major source of jobs. The construction industry is the second largest employer in the U.S.

Lightning Source UK Ltd.
Milton Keynes UK
UKHW050323110522
402791UK00005B/50